Did You

TAUNTON

A MISCELLANY

Compiled by Julia Skinner

With particular reference to the work of John Bainbridge

THE FRANCIS FRITH COLLECTION

www.francisfrith.com

First published in the United Kingdom in 2005 by The Francis Frith Collection®

This edition published exclusively for Bradwell Books in 2013
For trade enquiries see: www.bradwellbooks.com or tel: 0800 834 920
ISBN 978-1-84589-526-6

Text and Design copyright The Francis Frith Collection®
Photographs copyright The Francis Frith Collection® except where indicated.

The Frith® photographs and the Frith® logo are reproduced under licence from
Heritage Photographic Resources Ltd, the owners of the Frith® archive and trademarks.
'The Francis Frith Collection', 'Francis Frith' and 'Frith' are registered trademarks of
Heritage Photographic Resources Ltd.

All rights reserved. No photograph in this publication may be sold to a third party other than in the original
form of this publication, or framed for sale to a third party. No parts of this publication may be reproduced,
stored in a retrieval system, or transmitted, in any form, or by any means, electronic, mechanical, photocopying,
recording or otherwise, without the prior permission of the publishers and copyright holder.

British Library Cataloguing in Publication Data

Did You Know? Taunton - A Miscellany
Compiled by Julia Skinner
With particular reference to the work of John Bainbridge

The Francis Frith Collection
6 Oakley Business Park,
Wylye Road, Dinton,
Wiltshire SP3 5EU
Tel: +44 (0) 1722 716 376
Email: info@francisfrith.co.uk
www.francisfrith.com

Printed and bound in Malaysia
Contains material sourced from responsibly managed forests

Front Cover: **TAUNTON, EAST STREET 1902** 48724p

The colour-tinting is for illustrative purposes only, and is not intended to be historically accurate

AS WITH ANY HISTORICAL DATABASE, THE FRANCIS FRITH ARCHIVE IS CONSTANTLY BEING
CORRECTED AND IMPROVED, AND THE PUBLISHERS WOULD WELCOME INFORMATION ON
OMISSIONS OR INACCURACIES

CONTENTS

INTRODUCTION

Taunton lies at the very heart of Somerset, with the Quantock and Brendon Hills and Exmoor to the west and the low-lying marshes of the Somerset Levels to the east. This ancient borough takes its name from the River Tone, which winds through the town.

Many an English town has had brushes with England's history, but few can boast such an interesting record of conflict and rebellion as Taunton. The variety of important historical figures who passed this way, leaving a mark upon both local and national history, ranges from Saxon warlords to Norman conquerors, from ecclesiastical scholars to Tudor kings, from rebels to cloth-weavers. The story of Taunton is full of fascinating characters and events, of which this book can only provide a glimpse.

Taunton is the county town of Somerset and has thrived from its setting on the fertile plain of Taunton Deane. It was famous for agriculture and cloth production from medieval times, and even after the decline of the wool and cloth trade, agriculture helped to stave off hard times. The poet Michael Drayton asked: 'What ear so empty is this, they hath not heard the sound of Taunton's fruitful Deane?'

In mid Victorian times, old Taunton town began to change from its old medieval layout to much like the street pattern that we see today. This was the great age of civic reconstruction. Old churches were restored, in Taunton's case quite sympathetically, and new municipal buildings rose as fast as old insanitary slums were demolished. Whole new roads were laid out, such as the aptly-named Corporation Street. Railways brought new residents and visitors to Taunton, and modern industries were founded on the edge of town.

Did You Know?

TAUNTON

A MISCELLANY

Many of the old buildings seen in the old photographs in this book have survived, and it is still possible to walk around present-day Taunton to see the streets pictured in these views; it is in fact somewhat safer now, for both High Street and Fore Street have been pedestrianised, so the explorer is able to linger and compare scenes.

CORPORATION STREET 1935 86825

LOCAL DIALECT WORDS AND PHRASES

The nearby village of Norton Fitzwarren is believed to have earlier origins than Taunton itself. An old local rhyme goes:
'When Taunton was a furzey down, Norton was a market town'.

'Dimpsey' - twilight, dusk.

'Scrumpy' - cider.

'Scrumping' - stealing apples.

'Dumbledore' - bumble bee.

'Wha' be gwain 'ave?' - What are you going to have?

'Right nottlin' - very cold.

'Ruckles' - peat stacks.

'Muckers' - mates, friends.

'Athirt' - across.

'Backalong' - some time ago.

'Mommet' - a scarecrow, also used to describe a foolish or untidy person, ie ***'What a mommet of a maid!'***

HAUNTED TAUNTON

At Taunton Castle it is said that the tramp of James II's soldiers bringing the Duke of Monmouth's rebels to trial can still be heard in the corridors, and a sighting of a bewigged figure in late 17th-century clothes, wearing long boots and gauntlets and with a pistol in his hand, has been reported on a landing. Sightings of a fair-haired young woman in 17th-century dress have also been reported in the Great Hall of the castle, and there have been poltergeist manifestations.

A room at the Tudor Tavern is believed to be haunted, and a photograph of the supposed ghost appeared in The Field magazine on 15 October 1959.

A room in the Naval & Military Inn is supposed to be haunted. Three ghost hunters in the 20th century who investigated the room were scared away when the sounds of a ghostly argument became too much for their nerves to bear!

A spot on the A38 near Taunton is said to be haunted by two phantom hitchhikers. Most commonly reported is a man who stands by the roadside dressed in a long grey coat. If the driver of an approaching car does not slow down to offer him a ride, he throws himself in front of the vehicle. A female hitchhiker who does the same has also been reported in the area.

The area around the Upper High Street is said to be haunted by a ghost with green hair, supposed to be that of someone who died by drowning.

TAUNTON MISCELLANY

There is little evidence for much of a settlement on the site of present-day Taunton until the early 8th century, but the 'Anglo-Saxon Chronicle' relates that in AD722 Queen Aethelburg 'destroyed Taunton, which King Ine had formerly built'. The Taunton of King Ine's day would have been a collection of small thatched huts. It is likely that it was King Ine who gave the Saxon manor of Taunton to the See of Winchester - a connection that endured for several centuries. King Ine made Taunton his headquarters after his defeat of the local 'Welsh' inhabitants (an Anglo-Saxon term for the British), using it as a base to defend his embryonic kingdom of Wessex.

After the Norman Conquest, King William's great survey in 1086 of the value of his new lands, later known as the Domesday Book, gives interesting figures for the great estate known as the manor of Taunton Deane; this was possibly the largest manor in England, and included many individual villages in the area of Taunton as well as the emerging town. 265 labourers and peasant farmers ('villeins') worked the land belonging to the Bishop of Winchester, using some 60 ploughs between them; 70 of these men were bondmen, effectively indentured slaves. A further 64 burgesses or freemen lived in the growing town of Taunton itself. In addition there were 3 mills, worth 95 shillings a year, and a market which made an annual profit of 50 shillings. The town mint produced coinage to the profit of 50 shillings. These figures suggest a mostly Saxon population of around 1,600 people, dominated by a Norman militia and bureaucracy.

CASTLE SQUARE c1940 T16017

Photograph T16017, above, shows a glimpse through the Castle Bow towards the Castle Green. This area was once the site of a Saxon Minster and burial ground. In recent centuries the green was used for livestock markets.

During the 12th century there was a civil war in England between supporters of Matilda, the daughter and only surviving legitimate heir of Henry I, and her cousin, King Stephen, who had taken the throne. The period was known as the Anarchy, or the 'nineteen long winters' of King Stephen's reign. Parts of Taunton's castle date from this period, when Henry de Blois, half-brother of Stephen, fortified the town.

To the west of Taunton on the Somerset Levels is Athelney, the marshy area where King Alfred took refuge from the Danes in AD878 whilst he regrouped his forces. Photograph 57416, below, shows the Alfred Jewel - this famous object was found in 1693 near the site of Athelney Abbey. It is now kept in the Ashmolean Museum in Oxford. The jewel is made of gold and cloisonée enamel. The figure on the Jewel has been interpreted as either a representation of Christ as the Wisdom of God, or possibly a personification of Sight. The function of the Jewel is unknown, but it may have been one of the 'aestels', or book pointers, which we know that King Alfred sent to each bishopric in his realm with a copy of his own translation of Pope Gregory's 'Pastoral Care'. Alternatively it may have been a symbol of office, possibly sent by Alfred to one of his bishops or officials. The inscription on the jewel in Anglo-Saxon, 'Aelfred mec heht gewyrcan', means 'Alfred ordered me to be made'.

THE ALFRED JEWEL 1907 57416

Men from the Taunton area of the Anglo-Saxon kingdom of Wessex very probably made up part of King Alfred's army when it won an important victory against the Danes at the Battle of Edington in AD878. The events were chronicled by King Alfred's biographer Bishop Asser: 'The same year, [AD878] after Easter, King Alfred, with a few followers, made for himself a stronghold in a place called Athelney, and from thence sallied with his vassals and the nobles of Somersetshire, to make frequent assaults upon the pagans. Also, in the seventh week after Easter, he rode to the stone of Egbert, which is in the eastern part of the wood which is called Selwood, which means in Latin Silva Magna, the Great Wood, but in British Coit-mawr. Here he was met by all the neighbouring folk of Somersetshire, and Wiltshire, and Hampshire, who had not, for fear of the pagans, fled beyond the sea; and when they saw the king alive after such great tribulation, they received him, as he deserved, with joy and acclamations, and encamped there for one night. When the following day dawned, the king struck his camp, and went to Okely, where he encamped for one night. The next morning he removed to Edington, and there fought bravely and perseveringly against all the army of the pagans, whom, with the divine help, he defeated with great slaughter, and pursued them flying to their fortification. Immediately he slew all the men, and carried off all the booty that he could find without the fortress, which he immediately laid siege to with all his army; and when he had been there fourteen days, the pagans, driven by famine, cold, fear, and last of all by despair, asked for peace, on the condition that they should give the king as many hostages as he pleased, but should receive none of him in return, in which form they had never before made a treaty with any one. The king, hearing that, took pity upon them, and received such hostages as he chose; after which the pagans swore, moreover, that they would immediately leave the kingdom; and their king, Guthrum, promised to embrace Christianity, and receive baptism at King Alfred's hands.'
From 'The Life of King Alfred', composed around AD888 by Bishop Asser.
Translation by Dr J A Giles (London 1847).

THE MUNICIPAL BUILDINGS 1902 48727

THE MARKET PLACE 1886 19074

FORE STREET SOUTH c1940 T16030

In the late 15th century the imposter Perkin Warbeck claimed to be Prince Richard, one of the sons of Edward IV who had been imprisoned in the Tower of London and then 'disappeared', and rightful king instead of Henry VII. In 1497, Perkin Warbeck rode into Taunton with his army after failing to capture Exeter. It is possible that his claim to the throne was accepted by some of the people of Taunton, for later, when Warbeck was captured and brought back to Taunton to face the wrathful king, Henry VII, 50 of the townsfolk were fined over £440, a massive sum at the time, for supporting the rebellion.

The Somerset Cricket Museum is housed in Priory Barn, which was once one of the gatehouses into Taunton's Augustinian priory.

East Street was once part of the main highway from London to Exeter, and many a mailcoach and stagecoach passed this way. It is still one of Taunton's busiest streets and remains a thoroughfare for motor traffic.

East Street leads into East Reach beyond which, until the last century, was open countryside. The two streets were once separated by East Gate, the old boundary of Taunton Borough. The earliest reference to the East Gate is from the mid 12th century, but it may have dated from a much earlier period. The gate was probably destroyed during the Civil War.

THE PARADE, THE KINGLAKE MONUMENT 1912 64499

In 1685 the Duke of Monmouth, the Protestant illegitimate son of Charles II who rebelled against his uncle, the Catholic James II, was proclaimed king in Taunton. He was given a rapturous welcome by the townsfolk, a number of whom joined his sickle and scythe army on its way to final defeat on the marshes of Sedgemoor. Retribution for the 'Pitchfork Rebellion' was swift and merciless. The infamous Judge Jeffreys presided over a number of his 'Bloody Assizes' throughout the West Country, including one in the Great Hall of Taunton Castle. Judge Jeffreys tried 514 people at Taunton, of which 144 were sentenced to death and another 284 were sentenced to transportation to work on the sugar plantations of the West Indies. Some of those condemned to death later had their sentences commuted to transportation, but a number of rebels were hanged, drawn and quartered in Taunton, and their remains displayed around Somerset to remind people not to rebel against the king. The town paid a heavy price for its flirtation with treason.

The Tudor House in Fore Street (see photograph 64507, opposite) is even older than its name suggests, for it dates to the 14th century and is the most ancient building in the town after the castle. It was once owned by Sir William Portman, who escorted the Duke of Monmouth to London for his trial and execution following the Monmouth Rebellion. It has most recently seen service as a public house, the Tudor Tavern. In the heyday of Taunton market there were some 20 inns in this area of the town.

In the late 18th century the wool and cloth industry in Taunton declined but silk making was introduced into the town in 1778. In the later 19th century a new industry, making shirt collars, flourished. Other local industries included brewing and iron founding.

THE TUDOR HOUSE,
FORE STREET 1912 64507

EAST STREET 1902 48724

Photograph 48724 (above) shows a busy street scene in the second year of Edward VII's reign. It is still possible to see much the same scene today, although the styles of transport and fashion have changed. The buildings to the left of the photograph have survived, though all have acquired a change of use. The London Hotel was called the Three Cups Tavern in Tudor times, and was renamed the County Hotel in the early 20th century. The horse-bus in front of the portico was used to convey guests to and from the railway station. The alley to the right of the hotel building now leads to the New Market Shopping Centre.

Taunton is home to the world's leading supplier of paper charts and navigational publications to the marine sector, the UK Hydrographic Office.

One of the earliest boats in the country can be found in Taunton, at the County Museum. The dug-out canoe was found during excavations at the Meare lake village and dates from the Iron Age.

Vivary Park is so named because two fishponds - or vivaria - belonging to the Bishop of Winchester were to be found here in the Middle Ages. The impressive gates to the park, seen in photograph 55797, below, bear the legend 'Borough of Taunton' and the motto 'Defendamus', and were restored in 2001.

THE PARK GATES 1906 55797

The Castle Hotel is now two storeys higher than the building seen in photograph 4937, opposite. Famous guests here have included a Russian Tsar, the Emperor of Mexico, British royalty and the Duke of Wellington. In more recent years the Castle Hotel was famous for its Head Chef, a certain Gary Rhodes, who was here from 1986 to 1990.

The side-saddle traveller Celia Fiennes visited Taunton in 1698 and commented on the town: 'Taunton is a Large town haveing houses of all sorts of buildings both brick and stone, but mostly timber and plaister, its a very neate place and Looks substantial as a place of good trade. You meete all sorts of Country women wrapp'd up in the mantles Called West Country rockets, a Large mantle doubled together of a sort of serge, some are Linsywolsey and a deep fringe or ffag at the Lower End, these hang down some to their feete some only just below ye wast, in the summer they are all in white garments of this sort, in the winter they are in Red ones. I Call them garments because they never go out wth out them and this is the universal ffashion in Sommerset and Devonshire and Cornwall. Here is a good Market Cross well Carv'd and a Large Market house on Pillars for the Corn.'

THE CASTLE HOTEL c1869 4937

THE MARKET 1925 78812

ST MARY MAGDALENE'S CHURCH 1888 20859

The two traditional industries of Taunton Deane in medieval times were cloth production and agriculture. In a sense one was dependent on the other, for wool provided the raw material for the cloth, not least the rough serge known as 'Taunton Cloth'. The Pipe Rolls records of the Bishop of Winchester indicate that the cloth industry in Taunton dates from 1219 when a fulling mill was built north of the castle, and the Bishop purchased a number of sheep. Surnames such as Weaver, Clothier and Webb tell of local connections with the cloth trade.

The wealth that was created in Taunton in the Middle Ages by both agriculture and the cloth industry was often spent on the construction of fine buildings, especially churches, with their soaring towers. A Perpendicular Gothic architectural style of church towers developed in Somerset, which is distinctive enough for them to be known as 'Somerset Towers'. The 163ft-high tower of St Mary Magdalene's Church, built of Old Red Quantock sandstone and Ham Hill stone, dominates the skyline of Taunton. It is one of the most beautiful of many exquisite church towers in Somerset, despite being a reconstruction. The rebuild of the tower was completed in 1862, to the lines of the original 15th-century design.

The Grand Western Canal to Tiverton started from Taunton at Firepool, crossing Station Road by an aqueduct. The Grand Western was a 19th-century dream, planned to run from Taunton to the River Exe near Exeter. In the event, the main line from Taunton was built as a tub boat canal with a very short life, and an 11-mile stretch from Loudwells to Tiverton was built as a barge canal.

Vivary Park was purchased for the town in 1894, and a bandstand and the gates were added the following year. The park has been recently renovated with the help of a National Lottery grant. The fountain in the park, shown in photograph 64510, opposite, commemorates the life and reign of Queen Victoria. It was erected in 1907 and was paid for with £200 left over from funds raised to celebrate the coronation of Edward VII.

The Somerset Levels to the west of Taunton are one of the most important inland wetlands in Britain, if not the world. A very diverse range of wading birds and wildfowl can be seen in the Levels, and there is an RSPB reserve at Stathe.

Taunton has had a long connection with the military; a cavalry barracks was built as long ago as 1796. The Somerset Regiment saw action during the Napoleonic Wars and in most of the conflicts of the next two centuries. The Jellalabad Barracks were built in 1881 as a base for the Somerset Light Infantry, named after a place in Afghanistan where the soldiers had campaigned.

Photograph 64499 on page 13 shows the Kinglake Monument which commemorated Alexander William Kinglake, who served with Lord Raglan in the Crimea. The monument was demolished in the mid 20th century, much to the anger of the townsfolk.

VIVARY PARK, THE FOUNTAIN 1912 64510

THE BARRACKS 1894 34893

THE TAUNTON AND SOMERSET HOSPITAL 1902 48741

Taunton celebrated George III's Jubilee by building a new hospital for the town. It opened for patients in March 1812, with four wards and 26 beds. It was enlarged on several occasions throughout the Victorian period (see photograph 48741, above). A modern hospital at Musgrove Park now serves the needs of the people of Taunton.

In the book 'The Hitchhiker's Guide to the Galaxy' by Douglas Adams, Arthur Dent met Fenchurch at a pub in Taunton; although the pub was not actually named, it was described as being the pub closest to the station, which has been identified as the Railway Inn, now closed.

Taunton had neither a mayor nor a corporation for much of the 19th century: its affairs were administered by the Market Trust. However, a new charter was granted in 1877, and a mayor and a corporation were appointed. The Shire Hall (see photograph 4964, below) was built as a gesture towards municipal pride at the height of Victoria's reign. It stands on the former site of a large house called The Grove, once the home of Colonel Pearson, a local worthy.

There was probably some sort of crossing place over the Tone at Taunton in Saxon times, though the first recorded mention of a bridge was in 1280. By all accounts, Taunton's medieval bridge was an impressive six-span arched structure, though only 9ft 10ins at its narrowest point. The present bridge dates back only to 1896; it was strengthened in 1935, and repaired and renovated at the beginning of the 21st century.

THE SHIRE HALL c1869 4964

Taunton was not always the peaceful town we know today. Industrial disputes and rural rebellions sometimes brought conflicts and riots to its streets. On one occasion the

FORE STREET 1925 78807

spinners and weavers of Taunton raided the town gaol to
liberate colleagues who had been locked away after earlier
disturbances.

THE INDEPENDENT COLLEGE 1888 20869

Taunton School was founded as the Independent College in
the 1840s and was located in a street in the heart of the town.
The buildings shown in this photograph date from the 1870s
when the college relocated in search of more space to expand.
Independent College was renamed as Taunton School in 1899.

Many of the settlers of Taunton, Massachusetts in the USA were from Taunton in Somerset. This American Taunton was founded in 1637 by Elizabeth Poole, and was officially incorporated as a town in 1639. At the time of the incorporation the early settlers explained that they chose the name for their new settlement 'in honor and love to our dear native country ... And owning it a great mercy of God to bring us to this place, and settling of us, on lands of our own bought with our money in peace, in the midst of the heathen, for a possession for ourselves and for our posterity after us'. There is also another Taunton in the USA, in Minnesota.

One of the characters in the popular historical novel 'Lorna Doone', set on Exmoor, was the highwayman Tom Faggus. Tradition says that he was a real person, who was born at South Molton, and was hanged at Taunton. Faggus had a horse that was so well trained that it was believed to be his familiar spirit, and it was said that Faggus would never have been caught if his horse had not been shot first. There are no records to substantiate the story of Tom's execution in Taunton, and in the novel he meets a happier end: 'It was reported for a while that poor Tom had been caught at last, by means of his fondness for liquor, and was hanged before Taunton Jail; but luckily we knew better. With a good wife, and a wonderful horse, and all the country attached to him, he kept the law at a wholesome distance... Thereafter the good and respectable Tom lived a godly (though not always sober) life; and brought up his children to honesty, as the first of all qualifications.'

BISHOP'S HULL, THE VILLAGE 1906 55810

Bishop's Hull has maintained its identity, despite becoming a suburb of Taunton (see photograph 55810, above). Much open countryside remains to the west. The Church of St Peter and St Paul is unusual - it has one of Somerset's octagonal towers. Buried in the churchyard is William Crotch, a self-taught musical prodigy who became the first principal of the Royal Academy of Music in 1822.

An epitaph to a local doctor, recorded at West Monkton church, just outside Taunton:

> *Contention's doubtfull,*
> *Where two champions bee;*
> *Thou hast conquered Death,*
> *Now Death hath conquered thee.*

Taunton's castle was built as a motte and bailey castle in the early 12th century, and a tall stone keep was added later, when the castle was developed as a major military stronghold with walls 13ft thick. The gateway of the castle dates from 1495. The Municipal Hall was built between 1521 and 1522, and was the last addition to the castle, which was used as the administrative centre of the Bishop of Winchester's estate. The castle (with the town) was besieged during the Civil War, and Charles II ordered its destruction to prevent it being of military use to rebels in the future. The castle was restored by Sir Benjamin Hammet in the 18th century, and a museum opened there in 1778, which is now the Somerset County Museum.

EAST STREET c1940 T16028

In the Great Hall of Taunton Castle is a portrait by Sir Godfrey
Kneller of Lord Chief Justice Jeffreys, the 'Hanging Judge', one of the
most hated men in the West Country, who presided over his Bloody

Assizes in this very room. Also in the Great Hall is the Monmouth Cabinet, which contains artefacts from the Battle of Sedgemoor of 1685, which was the last battle fought on English soil.

EAST STREET 1929 82091

North of Taunton are the Quantocks, known to many students of English literature as the home for some years of the Romantic poets William Wordsworth and Samuel Taylor Coleridge. Coleridge and his wife lived at Nether Stowey, where he wrote his famous poems 'Kubla Khan', 'The Rime of the Ancient Mariner' and 'Frost at Midnight'. Wordsworth and his sister Dorothy lived for a short time at Alfoxton House at Holford, now a hotel, and loved to walk about the area: 'Upon smooth Quantock's airy ridge we roved'. Whilst Coleridge was living at Nether Stowey he came to the Unitarian Chapel in Taunton's Mary Street to preach on several occasions. Wordsworth's connections with the area are commemorated by several place names in Taunton, such as Wordsworth Drive.

The Bridgwater and Taunton Canal linked the River Parrett and the River Tone. The original intention was that the canal should extend to Exeter, but the coming of the railways made this plan uneconomic. The canal was built in the 1820s from a dock on the River Parrett at Huntworth to Taunton, and in 1842 was extended from Huntworth to a floating harbour north of Bridgwater, when the Huntworth dock was abandoned. The canal handled coal and slate from South Wales, but was unable to compete with the Great Western Railway after the Severn Tunnel was opened in 1886. The last commercial boats used the Bridgwater and Taunton Canal in the first decades of the 20th century. The canal was classified as a 'remainder waterway' (little more than a drainage channel) in the 1960s, but after the closure of Bridgwater Docks in 1971 efforts were made to restore the canal for leisure purposes. The towpath of the canal has been repaired and now forms part of the Sustrans cycle route NCR3, which connects Bath and Cornwall, and boating on the canal is encouraged. The canal is also part of the flood defences of the area, taking water from the River Tone at Taunton which is discharged into the Parrett at a sluice near Bridgwater.

THE CASTLE COURTYARD 1906 55795

NORTH STREET c1940 T16010

37

CHEAPSIDE c1940 T16027

FORE STREET 1906 56777

The Taunton area was being advertised as 'cider country' as early as 1584, and for centuries cider production was a key factor in the local economy. In 1894 over 24,000 acres of land around Taunton were being used as orchards. The Taunton Cider Company was set up in 1921 at Norton Fitzwarren to make cider on a commercial basis. The company expanded, acquiring other local cider-making companies, and is particularly known for Dry Blackthorn cider. Sadly, cider is no longer made at the Norton Fitzwarren site, as the company was bought out by Matthew Clark. However, traditional farmhouse cider is still made in Somerset by small-scale producers, and is well worth seeking out. The secret is in the blending of juice from several varieties of cider apples, many of which go by delightful names such as Slack-ma-girdle, Honey String, Buttery Door, and Poor Man's Profit.

In All Saints' Church at Norton Fitzwarren is a 16th-century rood screen noteworthy for its carvings, including that of a dragon. This may be a reference to a local legend which tells how a mighty dragon once terrorised the area, devouring children and destroying crops. A brave young man called Fulke Fitzwarren stood up to the dragon, and after a bitter fight he pierced the monster's heart with his sword, and cut off its head.

Taunton's double-decker trams eventually gave way to single-deckers, as seen in photograph 56777, opposite. The memorial cross also shown in this photograph is usually called the Burmese War Memorial. Now to be found in the Parade, the cross has marked upon it the battle honours of the Somerset Regiment, including Jellalabad (1841-42), Burma (1885), and South Africa (1899-1902). A 20th-century war memorial stands some distance away in Vivary Park.

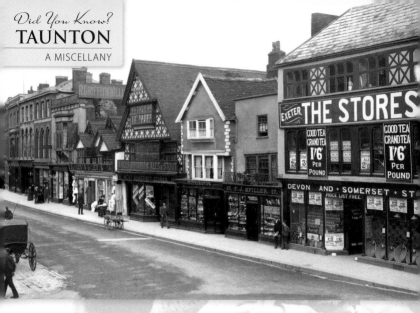

FORE STREET 1902 48723

The wetlands of the Somerset levels have a long tradition as a major willow growing and basket making area - the baskets seen in a shop window on the right of photograph 48723, above, were very probably made locally. The Willows & Wetlands Centre at the nearby village of Stoke St Gregory is a fascinating place to visit and learn about the cultivation of 'withies' and the traditional Somerset industries of basket making, willow weaving and hurdle making. 150 million plastic carrier bags are used in the United Kingdom every week, and a plastic bag can take up to 500 years to decay - why not support Somerset's basket makers and help the environment at the same time by using a willow basket for your shopping?

The Bearskin 'caps' of the Life Guards who guard royal residences and the Tower of London are constructed over a woven frame of Somerset willow.

The Taunton and Bridgwater Canal formed part of the Taunton Stop Line during the Second World War, a defensive line in south-west England designed 'to stop an enemy's advance from the west and in particular a rapid advance supported by armoured fighting vehicles (up to the size of a German medium tank) which may have broken through the forward defences'. The Taunton Stop Line was one of 50 such defensive lines all over the country; it ran for nearly 50 miles through Devon, Dorset and Somerset, from Axminster to Chard, Ilminster, Taunton, Bridgwater and Highbridge. The Stop Line was made up of natural obstacles such as rivers, canals and railway lines, and was defended by 309 light machine-gun pillboxes, 61 medium machine-gun emplacements, 21 anti-tank gun emplacements and other anti-tank obstacles such as concrete posts and pyramids. The line, which was supposed to slow down the enemy advance should German forces invade the country, as they were fully expected to do, was defended by two divisions from GHQ Home Forces Reserve, and, after 1940, the Home Guard. Many of the pillboxes can still be seen along the length of the line.

NORTH STREET 1925 78809

There was once a leper hospital in the Hamilton Road area, which was founded in the 12th century. In the Middle Ages the word 'hospital' meant a hospice or refuge. Leprosy became quite common in England at this time, and leper hospitals provided a home in isolation for sufferers from this dreadful disease, often with land which they could cultivate and a chapel where they could worship. Leper hospitals were often sited outside the town boundaries but close to roads so that the lepers could beg for alms from passers-by. Taunton's leper hospital was rebuilt in the 16th century as St Margaret's Almshouses, under the patronage of the Abbot of Glastonbury. In 1938 the building became the headquarters of the Somerset Guild of Craftsmen and Rural Community Council. In the late 1980s they moved elsewhere, and the building became derelict. The Somerset Building Preservation Trust then took on the building, and it has now been repaired.

The scene shown in photograph 48720, opposite, of the junction of Fore Street and East Street, has now changed considerably. The memorial cross has been relocated to the Parade, the trams are no more, and Fore Street has been pedestrianised. The carriage seen on the left of the photograph was the private conveyance of the London Hotel, just around the corner.

THE PARADE 1923 74033

FORE STREET 1902 48720

There are several Somerset folklore beliefs associated with willow trees, which grow widely on the Levels and are used for basket making. Willow twigs were often placed around the hearths of cottages for protection against evil and to bring good luck. There was also a belief that willow trees could move around, often following travellers, and could sometimes be heard muttering to themselves. An old rhyme went:

> *Ellum do grieve*
> *Oak he do hate,*
> *Willow do walk*
> *If you travels late.*

In most cider-making counties such as Somerset, a traditional ceremony known as wassailing (from the Anglo-Saxon 'Waes Hal', meaning 'good heath') was held in the winter, usually on Twelfth Night; jugs of cider were carried into the orchards, most of which would be drunk, and the rest would be poured around the roots of the apple trees. A lot of noise would be made with banging of pots and pans, to drive away evil spirits from the trees, and wake up the trees for the spring; sometimes shotguns would be fired through the branches. Special cakes would often be eaten, and pieces of cake or bread, soaked in cider, would be placed in the trees as a thanksgiving to the tree spirit, and to ensure a good crop in the following year.

In the Somerset County Museum at Taunton Castle is a Roman mosaic floor that is unique in Britain, in that its five panels make up a narrative story, making it one of the earliest examples of narrative art in the country. The Low Ham Roman Mosaic was found in 1946 during excavations on an unusually large villa at Low Ham in south-east Somerset. The panels depict the story of Aeneas and Dido, as told by the Roman poet Virgil in 'The Aeneid', which chronicles the adventures of Aeneas after he escaped from the fall of Troy. The mosaic was voted one of Britain's top Roman artefacts in a national poll in 2005 organised by Channel 4's 'Time Team' television programme.

SPORTING TAUNTON

It has been reported that in the late 19th century Taunton Rugby Football Club played night games away to Bridgwater illuminated by torches and flares on poles!

Taunton Town FC's greatest honour was winning the FA Vase. They beat Berkhamsted 2-1 at Villa Park in May 2001. The club also appeared at Wembley Stadium in May 1994, losing to Diss Town in the FA Vase final.

Taunton is the home of Somerset County Cricket Club. In 1946, M M Walford scored 100 in his first match for the county against India. He was the first player to do this at Taunton. Over the years the county ground has seen many fine players and teams, including of course the great Somerset side of the 1970s which included Ian Botham, Viv Richards and Joel Garner.

Taunton's most famous rugby-playing son is surely Andy Robinson. He was born in the town in 1964 and played eight times for England whilst a player at Bath RC. He was given the great honour of being made England National Rugby Coach in 2004.

Horse racing has a long but rather patchy history in Taunton. There have been several venues for racing in the area over the centuries, including Broomhay from 1788, as well as Mountlands, site of the present day King's College. The races also had a fifteen-year spell at Trull Moor. The current venue course, hosting National Hunt racing, has been open since 1927, and although nearly 80 years old it is the youngest course in the country holding National Hunt race meetings.

QUIZ QUESTIONS

Answers on page 50.

1. Who was spared having to eat a rather unappetising meal in 1645?

2. Who were 'Kirke's Lambs'?

3. What is the link between Taunton and 'The Canterbury Tales'?

4. When and why did a donkey admire the view from a church tower?

5. What is the connection between a small village not far from Taunton and the popular film 'Zulu'?

6. Who were 'The Maids of Taunton'?

7. With which French town is Taunton twinned?

8. What is the motto on the borough coat of arms, and what does it mean?

9. Where in Taunton can you find three little piggies?

10. The introduction of silk weaving into Taunton dates from 1778, when the industry was begun by Messrs Forbes & Wasedale. Silk is made by silkworms - what do silkworms eat?

THE COUNTY CRICKET GROUND 1902 48716

THE TOWN BRIDGE 1902 48734

RECIPE

TAUNTON TOAST

Ingredients
4 thick slices of bread
50g/2oz butter or margarine
1 level tablespoonful dry
English mustard

4 tablespoonfuls dry
Somerset cider
225g/8oz grated strong
Cheddar cheese
Salt and pepper to taste

Melt the butter in a saucepan over a gentle heat. Stir in the mustard, cider and cheese, and continue stirring until all the cheese has melted and the mixture is smooth and creamy. Season to taste.

Toast the bread, then spread the cheese mixture on the slices. Place them under a hot grill until golden brown and bubbling.

RECIPE

SOMERSET CIDER CAKE

Ingredients

250g/8oz mixed sultanas, raisins and currants

4 tablespoonfuls sweet Somerset cider

175g/6oz butter or margarine

175g/6oz soft brown sugar

3 eggs

250g/8oz self-raising flour

1 teaspoonful mixed spice (optional)

Soak the dried fruit in the cider overnight. Cream the butter or margarine and add the sugar. Cream until fluffy. Lightly beat the eggs and gradually beat them into the mixture. Mix in the fruit and cider. Sift the flour and spice together, fold in half of the flour, and mix well. Mix in the rest of the flour. Grease a 20cm/8-inch round or 18cm/7-inch square tin and line the bottom with greased, greaseproof paper. Bake in a moderate oven, 180 degrees C/350 degrees F/Gas Mark 4 for 1 hour and 10 minutes.

Did You Know?
TAUNTON
A MISCELLANY

QUIZ ANSWERS

1. The Parliamentarian Admiral Robert Blake, who defended Taunton against a prolonged Royalist siege in 1644-45 during the Civil War. He declared that he would eat his boots before he surrendered. The siege was relieved by the forces of Sir Thomas Fairfax, sparing Blake this indignity, and saving the town from the likelihood of destruction at the hands of the Royalist army. The resistance of Taunton almost certainly contributed to the eventual defeat of the king's army in the West Country.

2. 'Kirke's Lambs' was the ironic nickname given to the troops of Colonel Kirke because of their cruelty. After the Battle of Sedgemoor in 1685, Kirke's Lambs hunted down the rebels who had supported the Duke of Monmouth, a number of whom were summarily hanged at Taunton's High Cross. More Taunton rebels were later executed after being condemned at the Bloody Assizes.

3. An early constable of Taunton Castle was Thomas Chaucer, son of Geoffrey Chaucer, the author of 'The Canterbury Tales'.

4. During the rebuild of the tower of St Mary Magdalene's Church, a donkey powered the pulley which took up the stone to the workmen. When the work was completed in 1862, the donkey was taken up to the top of the tower to admire the view!

5. The south chancel window in the church at Hatch Beauchamp, just off the A358 between Taunton and Ilminster, is dedicated to John Chard VC, who died in the village. Chard was the commanding officer at the defence of Rorke's Drift in the Zulu Wars - he was immortalised in the popular film 'Zulu' about the engagement, in which he was played by the actor Stanley Baker.

6. The Duke of Monmouth arrived in Taunton in June 1685 and was proclaimed king there. A group of young Taunton girls, pupils of Mistress Susanna Musgrave and Mistress Mary Blake, presented Monmouth with banners which they had embroidered. After the Monmouth Rebellion failed, the girls were imprisoned as part of the savage retribution which was meted out to the West Country. Their relatives had to pay a heavy ransom for their release. A plaque commemorating the visit of the Duke of Monmouth can be seen at the bottom of Taunton's High Street.

7. Taunton is twinned with the French town of Lisieux in lower Normandy.

8. The motto is 'Defendamus', which means 'we shall defend'. This was recorded first in 1685, and is probably a reference to the Civil War siege of 1644-45 when Taunton refused to surrender to Royalist forces.

9. The area of the old Pig Market, which operated from 1614 to 1882, is marked with three wooden pigs.

10. The primary food source for silkworms is the leaves of mulberry trees.

FRENCH WEIR 1906 55800

FRANCIS FRITH

PIONEER VICTORIAN PHOTOGRAPHER

Francis Frith, founder of the world-famous photographic archive, was a complex and multi-talented man. A devout Quaker and a highly successful Victorian businessman, he was philosophical by nature and pioneering in outlook. By 1855 he had already established a wholesale grocery business in Liverpool, and sold it for the astonishing sum of £200,000, which is the equivalent today of over £15,000,000. Now in his thirties, and captivated by the new science of photography, Frith set out on a series of pioneering journeys up the Nile and to the Near East.

INTRIGUE AND EXPLORATION

He was the first photographer to venture beyond the sixth cataract of the Nile. Africa was still the mysterious 'Dark Continent', and Stanley and Livingstone's historic meeting was a decade into the future. The conditions for picture taking confound belief. He laboured for hours in his wicker dark-room in the sweltering heat of the desert, while the volatile chemicals fizzed dangerously in their trays. Back in London he exhibited his photographs and was 'rapturously cheered' by members of the Royal Society. His reputation as a photographer was made overnight.

VENTURE OF A LIFE-TIME

By the 1870s the railways had threaded their way across the country, and Bank Holidays and half-day Saturdays had been made obligatory by Act of Parliament. All of a sudden the working man and his family were able to enjoy days out, take holidays, and see a little more of the world.

With typical business acumen, Francis Frith foresaw that these new tourists would enjoy having souvenirs to commemorate their days out. For the next thirty years he travelled the country by train and by pony and trap, producing fine photographs of seaside resorts and beauty spots that were keenly bought by millions of Victorians. These prints were painstakingly pasted into family albums and pored over during the dark nights of winter, rekindling precious memories of summer excursions. Frith's studio was soon supplying retail shops all over the country, and by 1890 F Frith & Co had become the greatest specialist photographic publishing company in the world, with over 2,000 sales outlets, and pioneered the picture postcard.

FRANCIS FRITH'S LEGACY

Francis Frith had died in 1898 at his villa in Cannes, his great project still growing. By 1970 the archive he created contained over a third of a million pictures showing 7,000 British towns and villages.

Frith's legacy to us today is of immense significance and value, for the magnificent archive of evocative photographs he created provides a unique record of change in the cities, towns and villages throughout Britain over a century and more. Frith and his fellow studio photographers revisited locations many times down the years to update their views, compiling for us an enthralling and colourful pageant of British life and character.

We are fortunate that Frith was dedicated to recording the minutiae of everyday life. For it is this sheer wealth of visual data, the painstaking chronicle of changes in dress, transport, street layouts, buildings, housing and landscape that captivates us so much today, offering us a powerful link with the past and with the lives of our ancestors.

Computers have now made it possible for Frith's many thousands of images to be accessed almost instantly. The archive offers every one of us an opportunity to examine the places where we and our families have lived and worked down the years. Its images, depicting our shared past, are now bringing pleasure and enlightenment to millions around the world a century and more after his death.

For further information visit: www.francisfrith.com

INTERIOR DECORATION

Frith's photographs can be seen framed and as giant wall murals in thousands of pubs, restaurants, hotels, banks, retail stores and other public buildings throughout Britain. These provide interesting and attractive décor, generating strong local interest and acting as a powerful reminder of gentler days in our increasingly busy and frenetic world.

FRITH PRODUCTS

All Frith photographs are available as prints and posters in a variety of different sizes and styles. In the UK we also offer a range of other gift and stationery products illustrated with Frith photographs, although many of these are not available for delivery outside the UK – see our web site for more information on the products available for delivery in your country.

THE INTERNET

Over 100,000 photographs of Britain can be viewed and purchased on the Frith web site. The web site also includes memories and reminiscences contributed by our customers, who have personal knowledge of localities and of the people and properties depicted in Frith photographs. If you wish to learn more about a specific town or village you may find these reminiscences fascinating to browse. Why not add your own comments if you think they would be of interest to others? See **www.francisfrith.com**

PLEASE HELP US BRING FRITH'S PHOTOGRAPHS TO LIFE

Our authors do their best to recount the history of the places they write about. They give insights into how particular towns and villages developed, they describe the architecture of streets and buildings, and they discuss the lives of famous people who lived there. But however knowledgeable our authors are, the story they tell is necessarily incomplete.

Frith's photographs are so much more than plain historical documents. They are living proofs of the flow of human life down the generations. They show real people at real moments in history; and each of those people is the son or daughter of someone, the brother or sister, aunt or uncle, grandfather or grandmother of someone else. All of them lived, worked and played in the streets depicted in Frith's photographs.

We would be grateful if you would give us your insights into the places shown in our photographs: the streets and buildings, the shops, businesses and industries. Post your memories of life in those streets on the Frith website: what it was like growing up there, who ran the local shop and what shopping was like years ago; if your workplace is shown tell us about your working day and what the building is used for now. Read other visitors' memories and reconnect with your shared local history and heritage. With your help more and more Frith photographs can be brought to life, and vital memories preserved for posterity, and for the benefit of historians in the future.

Wherever possible, we will try to include some of your comments in future editions of our books. Moreover, if you spot errors in dates, titles or other facts, please let us know, because our archive records are not always completely accurate—they rely on 140 years of human endeavour and hand-compiled records. You can email us using the contact form on the website.

Thank you!

For further information, trade, or author enquiries please contact us at the address below:

The Francis Frith Collection, 6 Oakley Business Park, Wylye Road, Dinton, Salisbury, Wiltshire, England SP3 5EU.
Tel: +44 (0)1722 716 376 Fax: +44 (0)1722 716 881
e-mail: sales@francisfrith.co.uk **www.francisfrith.com**